21st Century
Basic Skills
Library

YOUR HEALTHY PLATE
OILS AND FATS

3

by Katie Marsico

Cherry Lake Publishing • Ann Arbor, Michigan

Published in the United States of America
by Cherry Lake Publishing
Ann Arbor, Michigan
www.cherrylakepublishing.com

Content Adviser: Theresa A. Wilson, MS, RD, LD, Baylor College of
Medicine, USDA/ARS Children's Nutrition Research Center, Houston, Texas

Photo Credits: Cover and page 1, ©Maram/Shutterstock, Inc.; page 4,
©Patty Orly/Shutterstock, Inc.; page 6, ©wiedzma/Shutterstock, Inc.;
page 8, ©aliisik/Shutterstock, Inc.; page 10, ©SunnyS/Shutterstock,
Inc.; page 12, ©H. Tuller/Shutterstock, Inc.; page 14, ©Monkey Business
Images/Shutterstock, Inc.; page 16, ©Ukrphoto/Dreamstime.com;
page 18, ©Avstudio/Dreamstime.com; page 20, ©Darren Baker/
Dreamstime.com.

Library of Congress Cataloging-in-Publication Data
Marsico, Katie, 1980–
    Your healthy plate. Oils and fats/by Katie Marsico.
        p. cm.—(21st century basic skills library. Level 3)
    Includes bibliographical references and index.
    ISBN 978-1-61080-351-9 (lib. bdg.)—ISBN 978-1-61080-358-8 (e-book)—
ISBN 978-1-61080-402-8 (pbk.)
    1. Lipids in human nutrition—Juvenile literature. 2. Food—Fat content—
Juvenile literature. I. Title. II. Title: Oils. III. Series.
    TX553.L5M37 2012
    612.3'97—dc23   2011035127

Cherry Lake Publishing would like to acknowledge
the work of The Partnership for 21st Century Skills.
Please visit www.21stcenturyskills.org for more information.

Printed in the United States of America
Corporate Graphics Inc.
January 2012
CLSP10

TABLE OF CONTENTS

What Are Oils and Fats?

Do you eat butter on toast? Do you put dressing on your salad?

These foods are made using **fat**. **Oils** are a **liquid** form of fat. Other fats are solid.

Fats can be found in fish and many other foods. Lard is a kind of fat that comes from pork.

Some parts of plants have oil in them, too. Seeds and nuts are two examples.

Why Do You Need Oils and Fats?

Oils and fats are not a **food group**.

Some fats, such as oils, are healthy for your body.

Solid fats are usually not healthy.

Some oils have good fat.

Good fats from oils keep your heart and blood healthy.

Good fats help protect your body against **diseases**.

Oils have **vitamin E** in them, too.

Vitamin E is good for your skin and hair.

Your body also uses vitamin E to help protect your heart.

How Often Should You Eat Oils and Fats?

You need only a little good fat from oil each day.

Too much oil is not healthy. It is not good for your heart!

Only eat butter and other solid fats once in a while.

What Is a Healthy Way to Add Oils to Your Diet?

You can eat a small handful of nuts.

You can also eat sunflower seeds. A slice of **avocado** is another healthy choice.

A lot of foods are cooked or flavored with oils.

Salad dressing is one example. Try dressings made with olive or other oils. These are healthier than creamy dressings.

Find healthy ways to add oils to your **balanced diet**. It can be tricky!

Ask an adult which foods with oils and fats are best for you.

Find Out More

BOOK

Cleary, Brian P., and Martin Goneau (illustrator). *Oils (Just a Bit) to Keep Your Body Fit: What Are Oils?* Minneapolis: Millbrook Press, 2011.

WEB SITE

United States Department of Agriculture (USDA)—What Are Oils?
www.choosemyplate.gov/foodgroups/oils.html
Learn more about what oils are and how to add them to your diet.

Glossary

avocado (ah-vuh-KAH-doh) a pear-shaped fruit with green or black skin

balanced diet (BAL-uhntzt DYE-it) eating just the right amounts of different foods

diseases (di-ZEEZ-uhz) conditions that cause health problems

fat (FAT) oil found in certain kinds of foods

food group (FOOD GROOP) a group of different foods that people should have in their diets

liquid (LIH-kwid) something that flows and can be poured

oils (OYLZ) liquid forms of fat

vitamin E (VYE-tuh-min E) a substance that your body uses to help protect your skin and nails and to prevent heart disease

Home and School Connection

Use this list of words from the book to help your child become a better reader. Word games and writing activities can help beginning readers reinforce literacy skills.

a	choice	food	kind	other	these
add	comes	foods	lard	parts	to
adult	cooked	for	liquid	plants	toast
against	creamy	form	little	pork	too
also	day	found	lot	protect	tricky
an	diet	from	made	put	try
and	diseases	good	many	salad	two
another	do	group	much	seeds	uses
are	dressing	hair	need	should	using
as	dressings	handful	not	skin	usually
ask	each	have	nuts	slice	vitamin
avocado	eat	healthier	of	small	ways
balanced	example	healthy	often	solid	what
be	examples	heart	oil	some	which
best	fat	help	oils	such	while
blood	fats	how	on	sunflower	why
body	find	in	once	than	with
butter	fish	is	one	that	you
can	flavored	keep	only	them	your

Index

About the Author

Katie Marsico is an author of nonfiction books for children and young adults. She lives outside of Chicago, Illinois, with her husband and children.

mL

3-12